LIGHTHOUSES

Eagle Harbor Lighthouse, Lake Superior, Keweenaw County, Michigan

BROWNTROUT PUBLISHERS, INC.   P.O. BOX 280070   SAN FRANCISCO, CA 94128

LIGHTHOUSES

A BOOK
OF
30 POSTCARDS

BROWNTROUT PUBLISHERS INC.
SAN FRANCISCO

BROWNTROUT PUBLISHERS, INC.
P.O. BOX 280070
SAN FRANCISCO, CALIFORNIA 94128

ISBN: 1-56313-754-2
BROWNTROUT TITLE #B754

BROWNTROUT PUBLISHERS publishes a wide variety of books and calendars.
Please write for more information.

Printed in Korea

LIGHTHOUSES

Pigeon Point Lighthouse, California

BROWNTROUT PUBLISHERS, INC.   P.O. BOX 280070   SAN FRANCISCO, CA 94128

LIGHTHOUSES

Old Hereford Inlet Lighthouse, Wildwood, New Jersey

BROWNTROUT PUBLISHERS, INC.   P.O. BOX 280070   SAN FRANCISCO, CA 94128

LIGHTHOUSES

Ponce Inlet Lighthouse, Daytona Peninsula, Florida

BROWNTROUT PUBLISHERS, INC.   P.O. BOX 280070   SAN FRANCISCO, CA 94128

LIGHTHOUSES

Robert H. Manning Memorial Lighthouse, Lake Michigan, Empire, Michigan

BROWNTROUT PUBLISHERS, INC.   P.O. BOX 280070   SAN FRANCISCO, CA 94128

LIGHTHOUSES

Point Pinos Lighthouse, Pacific Grove, California

BROWNTROUT PUBLISHERS, INC.   P.O. BOX 280070   SAN FRANCISCO, CA 94128

LIGHTHOUSES

Marblehead Lighthouse at sunset, Lake Erie, Ohio

BROWNTROUT PUBLISHERS, INC.   P.O. BOX 280070   SAN FRANCISCO, CA 94128

LIGHTHOUSES

Holland Harbor Lighthouse at dawn, Lake Michigan, Holland, Michigan

BROWNTROUT PUBLISHERS, INC.   P.O. BOX 280070   SAN FRANCISCO, CA 94128

LIGHTHOUSES

Hunting Island Lighthouse, Hunting Island State Park, South Carolina

BROWNTROUT PUBLISHERS, INC. P.O. BOX 280070 SAN FRANCISCO, CA 94128

LIGHTHOUSES

Kewaunee Pierhead Lighthouse, Lake Michigan, Kewaunee, Wisconsin

BROWNTROUT PUBLISHERS, INC.   P.O. BOX 280070   SAN FRANCISCO, CA 94128

LIGHTHOUSES

Fort Amherst Lighthouse, Prince Edward Island

BROWNTROUT PUBLISHERS, INC.   P.O. BOX 280070   SAN FRANCISCO, CA 94128

LIGHTHOUSES

Trinidad Memorial Lighthouse, Trinidad, California

BROWNTROUT PUBLISHERS, INC.   P.O. BOX 280070   SAN FRANCISCO, CA 94128

LIGHTHOUSES

Big Sable Point Lighthouse, Lake Michigan, Mason County, Michigan

BROWNTROUT PUBLISHERS, INC.   P.O. BOX 280070   SAN FRANCISCO, CA 94128

LIGHTHOUSES

Place du Phare, La Matre, Gaspésie, Québec

BROWNTROUT PUBLISHERS, INC.   P.O. BOX 280070   SAN FRANCISCO, CA 94128

LIGHTHOUSES

Lighthouse at Pemaquid Point, Maine

BROWNTROUT PUBLISHERS, INC.   P.O. BOX 280070   SAN FRANCISCO, CA 94128

LIGHTHOUSES

Portland Head Lighthouse, Portland, Maine

BROWNTROUT PUBLISHERS, INC.   P.O. BOX 280070   SAN FRANCISCO, CA 94128

LIGHTHOUSES

Nauset Lighthouse, Eastham, Massachusetts

BROWNTROUT PUBLISHERS, INC.   P.O. BOX 280070   SAN FRANCISCO, CA 94128

LIGHTHOUSES

White River Lighthouse, Lake Michigan, Muskegon County, Michigan

BROWNTROUT PUBLISHERS, INC. P.O. BOX 280070 SAN FRANCISCO, CA 94128

LIGHTHOUSES

North Point Lighthouse, Lake Michigan, Two Rivers, Wisconsin

BROWNTROUT PUBLISHERS, INC.   P.O. BOX 280070   SAN FRANCISCO, CA 94128

LIGHTHOUSES

Cape Neddick Nubble Light, Maine

BROWNTROUT PUBLISHERS, INC.   P.O. BOX 280070   SAN FRANCISCO, CA 94128

LIGHTHOUSES

Cape Lookout Lighthouse, Cape Lookout National Seashore
off Harker's Island, North Carolina

BROWNTROUT PUBLISHERS, INC.   P.O. BOX 280070   SAN FRANCISCO, CA 94128

LIGHTHOUSES

Bass Harbor Lighthouse, Acadia National Park, Maine

BROWNTROUT PUBLISHERS, INC. .P.O. BOX 280070 SAN FRANCISCO, CA 94128

LIGHTHOUSES

Cape Henry Lighthouse, Virginia Beach, Virginia

BROWNTROUT PUBLISHERS, INC.   PO. BOX 280070   SAN FRANCISCO, CA 94128

LIGHTHOUSES

St. Marks Lighthouse, Apalachee Bay, Gulf of Mexico, Florida

BROWNTROUT PUBLISHERS, INC. P.O. BOX 280070 SAN FRANCISCO, CA 94128

LIGHTHOUSES

Lighthouse, Mystic River, Mystic Seaport, Connecticut

BROWNTROUT PUBLISHERS, INC. P.O. BOX 280070 SAN FRANCISCO, CA 94128

LIGHTHOUSES

Lighthouse, Fort Casey Historical State Park, Whidbey Island, Washington

BROWNTROUT PUBLISHERS, INC. P.O. BOX 280070 SAN FRANCISCO, CA 94128

LIGHTHOUSES

Marquette Harbor Lighthouse, Lake Superior, Marquette, Michigan

BROWNTROUT PUBLISHERS, INC.   P.O. BOX 280070   SAN FRANCISCO, CA 94128

LIGHTHOUSES

Umpqua River Lighthouse, Reedsport, Oregon

BROWNTROUT PUBLISHERS, INC. P.O. BOX 280070 SAN FRANCISCO, CA 94128

LIGHTHOUSES

Split Rock Lighthouse, Lake Superior, Minnesota

BROWNTROUT PUBLISHERS, INC.   P.O. BOX 280070   SAN FRANCISCO, CA 94128

LIGHTHOUSES

Assateague Lighthouse, Chincoteague National Wildlife Refuge, Virginia

BROWNTROUT PUBLISHERS, INC. P.O. BOX 280070 SAN FRANCISCO, CA 94128